Endpapers: (left) Shield, Mandan, painted hide,
Museum of the American Indian, Heye Foundation;
(right) Shield, Crow, painted hide,
National Museum of Natural History, Smithsonian Institution

Pipe bowl, Cheyenne, stone, Denver Art Museum,
photograph by Alfred Tamarin

THE ART OF THE
PLAINS INDIANS

Shirley Glubok

Designed by Gerard Nook · Special Photography by Alfred Tamarin

Macmillan Publishing Co., Inc.
New York
Collier Macmillan Publishers
London

The author gratefully acknowledges the assistance of:
Donald Baird, Curator, Princeton Museum of Natural History; *Tom Brown*, Museum of the Plains Indian;
Hugh A. Dempsey, Director of History, Glenbow-Alberta Institute; *Patty Harjo*, Conservator,
Anthropology Department, Denver Museum of Natural History; *Myles Libhart*, Director of Museums,
Exhibitions and Publications, Indian Arts and Crafts Board; *Les Stinn*, Ethnology Department,
Glenbow-Alberta Institute; *Eric C. Waterton*, Curator of Ethnology, Provincial Museum of Alberta;
Joe Ben Wheat, Curator, University of Colorado Museum; *Hilary Caws*;
and especially the helpful cooperation of *Richard Conn*,
Curator, Department of Native Arts, The Denver Art Museum

Other books by Shirley Glubok:

THE ART OF ANCIENT EGYPT
THE ART OF LANDS IN THE BIBLE
THE ART OF ANCIENT GREECE
THE ART OF THE NORTH AMERICAN INDIAN
THE ART OF THE ESKIMO
THE ART OF ANCIENT GREECE
THE ART OF AFRICA
ART AND ARCHAEOLOGY
THE ART OF ANCIENT PERU
THE ART OF THE ETRUSCANS
THE ART OF ANCIENT MEXICO
KNIGHTS IN ARMOR
THE ART OF INDIA
THE ART OF JAPAN
THE ART OF COLONIAL AMERICA
THE ART OF THE SOUTHWEST INDIANS
DOLLS DOLLS DOLLS

THE ART OF THE OLD WEST
THE ART OF THE NEW AMERICAN NATION
THE ART OF THE SPANISH IN THE
   UNITED STATES AND PUERTO RICO
THE ART OF CHINA
THE ART OF AMERICA FROM JACKSON TO LINCOLN
THE ART OF AMERICA IN THE GILDED AGE
THE ART OF AMERICA IN THE EARLY
   TWENTIETH CENTURY
THE ART OF THE NORTHWEST COAST INDIANS
THE FALL OF THE AZTECS
THE FALL OF THE INCAS
DISCOVERING TUT-ANKH-AMEN'S TOMB
DISCOVERING THE ROYAL TOMBS AT UR
DIGGING IN ASSYRIA
HOME AND CHILD LIFE IN COLONIAL DAYS

Cover illustration: Painted elk skin, Shoshone,
The Brooklyn Museum, Dick S. Ramsay Fund

Macmillan Publishing Co., Inc., 866 Third Avenue, New York, N.Y. 10022
Collier Macmillan Canada, Ltd.
Printed in the United States of America

1 2 3 4 5 6 7 8 9 10

Library of Congress Cataloging in Publication Data
Glubok, Shirley.   The art of the Plains Indians.
1. Indians of North America—Great Plains—Art—
Juvenile literature. [1. Indians of North America—
Great Plains—Art] I. Title.
E78.G73G58   709'.01'1   75-14064   ISBN 0-02-736360-0

By Mato-tope, 1833
(facsimile by Karl Bodmer),
Mandan, Northern Natural
Gas Company Collection, Joslyn
Art Museum, Omaha, Nebraska

The vast heartland of the North American continent, extending from the Mississippi River west to the Rocky Mountains, from Texas north into Canada, was once a natural pasture for huge herds of wild animals, especially American bison, commonly called buffalo. In ancient times very few people inhabited this area, known as the Great Plains. Now and then a few Indian hunters would cross the grasslands on foot in search of animals for food.

Travel became easier in the eighteenth century when horses, which had been brought to America by Spaniards who settled in the Southwest, reached the Plains. Now bands of Indians on horseback streamed out onto the Great Plains. They lived as nomads, or wanderers, and followed the buffalo year round.

Buffalo provided the Indians with everything they needed: meat for food, skins for tipis and clothing, bones and horns for tools, spoons and ornaments, and even hair for ropes. The skins of these animals were often painted and worn wrapped around the body as robes. The hides of fully grown buffalo cows or young bulls made excellent robes for adults; those of calves were worn by children. The Sioux woman at right wears a robe painted with a border-and-box design.

Colors used to paint the hides came from earth, plants and trees. They were ground to a powder, then mixed with a gluey substance so that the colors would stick to the surface. The glue was made by boiling the tail of a beaver or scrapings from animal hides. The colors were applied with sticks chewed at one end or bones, especially bones from the leg of the buffalo, which are spongy and hold paint yet can be sharpened to a fine point. After fur traders arrived in the area in the early nineteenth century, commercial colors were used.

Karl Bodmer, 1833, Northern
Natural Gas Company
Collection, Joslyn Art Museum

Only men were allowed to paint and wear buffalo hides decorated with figures

of people and animals. The hide robes of warriors told of the owners' successful

battles and horse raids. It was considered honorable and brave to capture horses

by raiding enemy tribes and, later, white settlements. This Cheyenne robe is painted

with the story of a horse raid. Some of the horses are represented by just their heads.

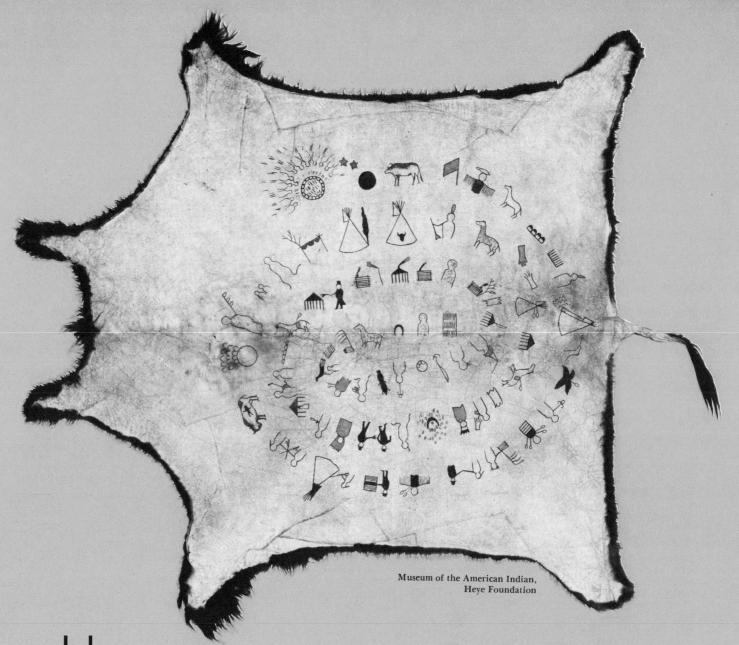

Hides were painted to record the history of a tribe. The Sioux called these records winter counts. They kept time by winters and would say that a person was so many snows old. Each figure stood for the most important event of a year.

The winter count above belonged to Lone Dog, a Sioux. It begins with the year 1800-1801, when thirty members of the tribe were killed by Crow Indians, as shown by three groups of ten lines in the center row of figures. Reading from right to left in that row, the head and body of a man covered with spots means that many Sioux died of smallpox in 1801–1802. The next year a Sioux captured white men's horses, as shown by the horseshoe. In 1803–1804 horses were captured from Crow Indians. Then the Sioux held a ceremonial pipe dance and went to war, as shown by the long pipestem ornamented with feathers. The symbols continue outward in a spiral, representing the events of seventy-one years.

The picture story at right, by a Blackfeet artist, was painted on cloth obtained by trade. It shows Blackfeet warriors capturing enemy horses. The designs on the tipis tell us that they are raiding a Cree Indian camp.

Child's Lodge, Piegan, photograph by Edward S. Curtis, 1910, Library of Congress

Tipis were painted with designs that came to the owner in a dream or vision. These designs were believed to give protection from sickness and misfortune. They belonged to the owner and were not to be copied by others.

In the days when buffalo were plentiful, tipi covers were made from buffalo skins that were cut up and sewn together into a semicircular shape. From six to twenty skins were used, depending on the size of the tipi. The cover was joined together by wooden pins over the entrance, which usually faced east, the direction of the sunrise. Wooden pegs fastened the tipi to the ground. These portable houses were easy to put up, take down and transport. Women were responsible for these chores. Men were responsible for the designs on the tipis.

Blackfeet, early twentieth century, Field Museum of Natural History, Chicago

Photograph by
Philip H. Godsell,
1949, Glenbow-
Alberta Institute,
Calgary, Alberta

10

The tipi structure is supported by three or four main poles tied together at the top, with as many as twenty other poles resting against them. Outside the tipi two separate, movable poles are attached to flaps at the top. The flaps can be opened to let smoke out, or closed to keep out rain.

The three tipis at left were made by the Blood, a division of the Blackfeet. They are painted with deer, buffalo and striped designs. The round forms at the base represent the earth and "fallen stars." Some designs were outlined while the tipis were standing. Then the covers were spread flat on the ground while the paintings were finished. In the old days a buffalo tail or a handful of long buffalo hair might be used to paint large surfaces. The whole family often helped to paint a tipi.

The covers of these Blood tipis are canvas, which was used when animal skins were no longer available. About fifty to seventy million buffalo roamed the Plains in the eighteenth century, but in the late nineteenth century they were almost all killed off. Originally, Indians had hunted them only for food, using their hides for shelter and clothing. But traders wanted their skins for sale and white settlers wanted the land on which the buffalo grazed,so more and more animals were killed. By the 1880's the buffalo was practically extinct.

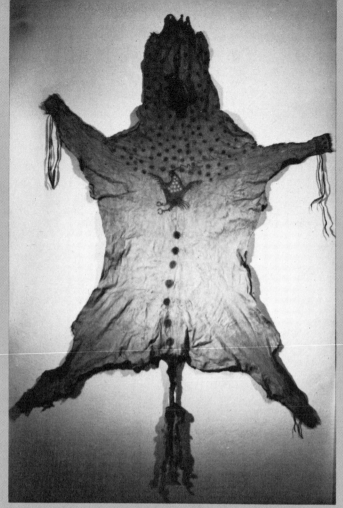

Provincial Museum of Alberta, photograph by Alfred Tamarin

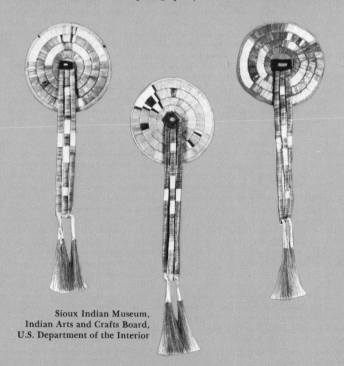

This buffalo-calf skin, painted with the design of a thunderbird, was used to cover the entrance to the tipi of Wolf Collar, a Blackfeet warrior. One night in August, 1870, he dreamed that Thunder came to him, first as a bird, then as a woman, took him into her tipi and gave him a drum with four songs. She also gave him the power to heal people who had been struck by lightning by rubbing a mixture of yellow paint and wet clay on the injured person's chest and singing the songs. Then she gave him permission to paint his tipi like her Thunder Lodge, and gave him three more songs. "Distant cloud hears me. Distant rain hears me. I want rain" was a song for the tipi.

The ornaments at left, made of deerskin and decorated with porcupine quills, were sewn onto the outside of a Sioux tipi. North American Indian women were the only people in the world to do quillwork.

An Arapaho story tells of a woman who chased a porcupine to get its quills. It ran up

a tree and she climbed after it. As she neared the top the tree grew taller, until it

reached the sky. Then the porcupine put her under its spell and took her into its camp

circle to live. She finally escaped by digging a hole and letting herself down to earth

on a long rope.

Large pieces of buffalo skin were sewn together and hung on the back wall inside

a tipi to give extra protection against drafts. The tipi lining below tells of the battles

of Red Bird, a Cheyenne chief, with the United States cavalry and his Indian enemies.

Red Bird is shown wearing a long, flowing, feathered war bonnet.

Southern Plains Indian Museum,
Indian Arts and Crafts Board,
U.S. Department of the Interior

War bonnets made of eagle feathers were worn in battle as magical protection against arrows and bullets. To the Plains Indians, feathers, especially those of the eagle, have religious meaning. When an eagle was killed, a ceremony took place to ask the bird's spirit for forgiveness. Feathered headdresses were a sign of high military rank and were worn in peace and war on special occasions.

At left Wa-shi-ta-ton-ga, or American Horse, an Oglala Sioux, is wearing his splendid, flowing war bonnet that reaches all the way to the ground. He is also wearing a fine shirt and a breastplate of long, narrow beads called hair pipes, which are made from leg bones or shells. His leggings, which reach from the ankles to the hips, are closed by laces along the

Photograph by William Henry Jackson, about 1877, State Historical Society of Colorado outer sides of the legs. They are supported by a strap fastened to a belt.

A "straight-up" bonnet, in which the feathers stand upright, is worn by Mrs. Big Knife, a Sarcee. The straight-up bonnet was considered sacred and was kept in a special tube-shaped container.

Mrs. Big Knife is wearing a cape with hundreds of thousands of trade beads sewn onto the cloth. Since the Plains Indians were nomads, they did not raise sheep, grow cotton or weave. The only cloth they had was obtained by trade. Big Knife, her husband, owned about a thousand horses, the largest number in his band. Horses were so valuable to the Indians that a man's wealth and importance were measured by the number that he owned.

Early 1920's,
Glenbow-Alberta Institute

A famous Blackfeet chief, Big Snake, wears a straight-up bonnet as he tells his chieftains of his war deeds in the painting above. Each chieftain wears a different style of feathered headdress or hairdo. Big Snake is holding a lance, or spear, and a shield decorated with feathers. The chieftain at far left wears a splendid painted buffalo robe with the hair on the inside for extra warmth. Several of the men have paint on their faces. Painting and tattooing, like earrings and nose rings, added to a person's beauty. Tattoo marks were made by pricking or cutting the skin and inserting color. It was so painful that drumming, rattling and singing took place during the operation to drown out any possible groans.

Photograph by Philip H. Godsell, 1949, Glenbow-Alberta Institute

All of the men are wearing shirts made of animal skin, with fringes and porcupine-quill decorations. Shirts worn by Plains Indian men were made from two animal skins, usually deer, bighorn or antelope. The skins were sewn together at the shoulders and sleeves were added.

A split horn headdress is worn by Robert Crow Eagle, of the North Piegan, a Blackfeet band. He was the grandson of Crow Eagle, who signed a treaty in 1877 by which Indians of southern Alberta turned over a vast area of land to the Canadian government. The horns on Robert Crow Eagle's headdress are wrapped with ribbon and trimmed with features and bells. Weasel skins, which were a sign of brave deeds in battle, hang from the rim. Bonnets of this type were usually worn by people who were instructed to wear them in a dream or vision.

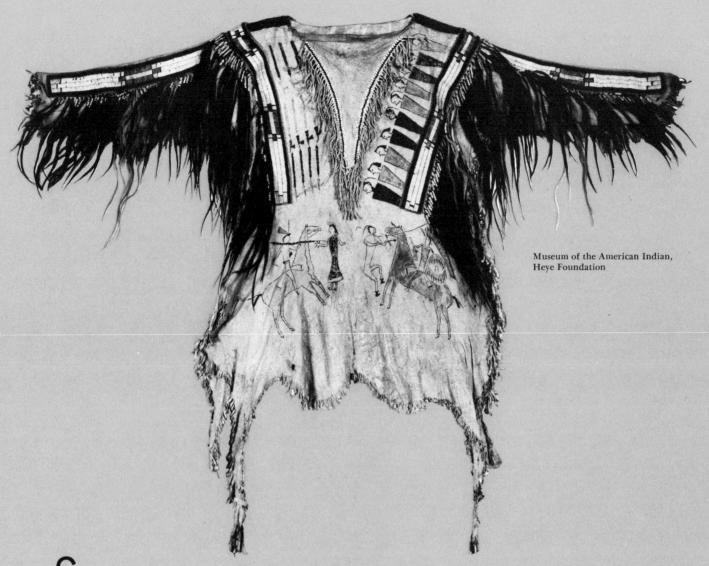

Shirts worn in war were often painted with designs to protect the warrior. The designs came to the owner in a vision. The Cheyenne painted buckskin shirt above is decorated with porcupine quills, beads and hair locks. Locks of human hair were proof of enemies slain in battle and were considered war trophies.

Indians of the Plains wore moccasins, which are soft, comfortable and sturdy. Some moccasins were made from a single piece of soft animal skin. Others were made in three pieces, the hard sole of rawhide and the upper part and tongue of soft leather.

Rawhide is stiff, sturdy animal skin, often from buffalo, which has not been tanned to make it into leather. The skin would be soaked in water and ashes for a day to loosen the hair, if it was to be removed. After this, the skin was stretched out flat and the hair and flesh scraped off with a bone or antler scraper before it was staked down to dry for several days. Drying shrank the skin, so it was then restretched. Finally, it was scraped to an even thickness with a sharp tool.

To turn this rawhide into soft leather, it was rubbed with an oily mixture of fat and animal brains, and polished by rubbing with a pebble. Then it was rolled into a bundle and pulled through a loop of sinew over and over again. Sinew came from cords along the buffalo's upper spine. After they were cleaned and dried, they were separated into fibers. Sinews were used for bowstrings, snowshoes and ropes, as well as for sewing.

The low, beaded men's moccasins are Sioux. The women's boots are Cheyenne. Although moccasins were made in much the same way throughout the Plains, each tribe had its own style of quill and bead-work designs.

19

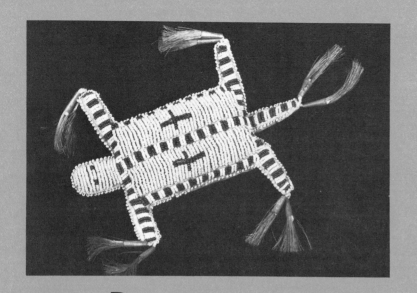 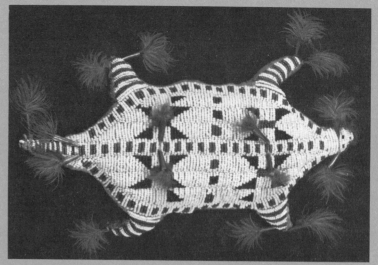

Beads obtained from traders were used to cover small pouches in the form of turtles or lizards. When a baby was born, his navel cord would be placed in a pouch and tied to his cradle as protection against sickness. After the baby learned to walk, the pouch was worn on a belt at his waist. The lizards with horsehair and feather tassels are both Sioux.

Plains Indian babies were carried about by their mothers in cradles strapped to their backs. The baby was held upright and could see the world from a high position. The cradle could be hung from a tree while the mother was working and she could attach it to her saddle when riding a horse. The baby's grandmother often decorated the cradle with porcupine quills or beads.

The designs on the Arapaho cradle, near right, were made with porcupine quills. For quillwork, the porcupines were plucked and the quills carefully sorted by size and put into bags. The women soaked them to soften them and flattened them with their teeth or fingernails before sewing them down. Before commercial dyes were available, porcupine quills were dyed by boiling them with plants.

The Cheyenne cradle in the center is attached to a wooden frame decorated with brass studs. The Crow cradle, below right, is fully beaded.

Before the women had needles for sewing, they attached the beads or quills by punching holes in the skins with an awl, a sharp instrument made of bone, and pushing the sinew through.

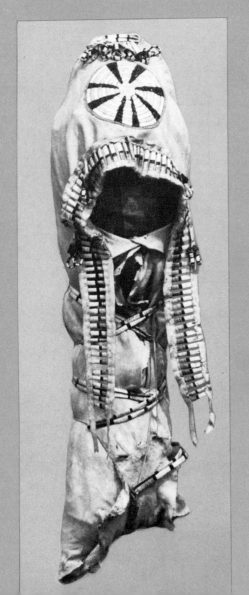
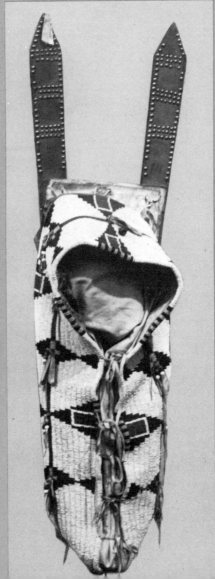
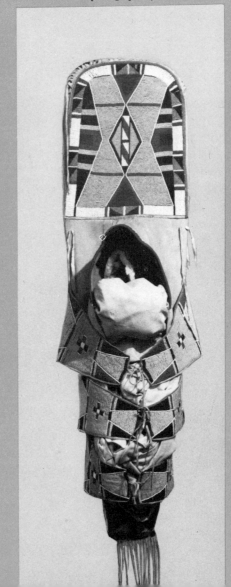

21

Provincial Museum of Alberta, photograph by Alfred Tamarin

On hunts or in warfare Plains Indians rode bareback and used the least possible amount of equipment. But for moving camp, visiting neighboring tribes, celebrations or parades they proudly decorated their horses with ornaments. Fancy trappings were a sign of wealth and high rank.

The horse at left is wearing Blackfeet ornaments of fine beadwork. The painted rawhide container with long fringes that hangs from the saddle is a case to hold a feathered bonnet or other ceremonial objects. Tipi poles are tied together over the horse's neck to drag a travois. A Blackfeet woman moving camp would use a large saddle, probably made of wood covered with rawhide. Men's saddles were usually pads, made of two pieces of hide and stuffed with deer or buffalo hair. Skin blankets were placed under saddles to protect the horse's back. The Sioux mask at right, with porcupine quillwork, covered a horse's face.

Museum of the Plains Indian,
Indian Arts and Crafts Board,
U.S. Department of the Interior

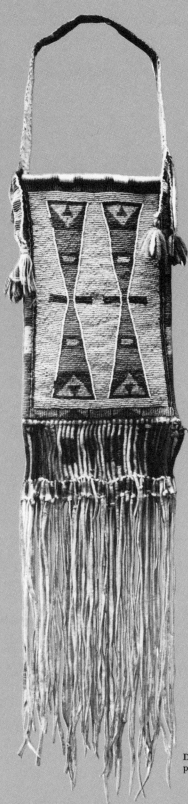

Glenbow-Alberta Institute

The Plains Indians needed lightweight, unbreakable, water-

proof containers in which to store their belongings. Tribes such as

the Mandan, who lived in earth-covered lodges on the prairies at

the edge of the Plains, did some farming and only went out on the

Plains in season to hunt. They made and used pottery. But pots or

Denver Art Museum,
photograph by Alfred Tamarin

even baskets were not practical for the nomadic Indians, who moved about on horseback all the time. They made flat rawhide containers that could be easily packed on horses.

The containers were useful for storing clothing, berries, dried roots and pemmican, a nutritious and long-lasting food that was light and easy to carry. Pemmican was made by cutting buffalo meat into thin strips, then drying it in the sun and mixing it with grease and dried berries.

Small personal possessions were carried by men and women in pouches tied to their belts. The Crow beaded bag at far left was made to hold a young man's face paint, comb, hairbrush, perfumed greases to keep his hair in place, mirror and tweezers for plucking the hairs on his face.

The painted bag with long fringes was made by the Piegan. Containers with fringes usually hold sacred objects.

Skin bags were also made to hold men's pipes and tobacco. On the long Cheyenne pipe bag at right, tiny beads are sewn closely together to form pictures of men and animals.

Denver Art Museum,
photograph by Alfred Tamarin

One of the most important possessions of a Plains Indian man was his shield, which offered magical as well as physical protection. The painted design, which had supernatural power, came to the owner in a dream or vision. Feathers and bones, strips of cloth and other hanging objects were thought to offer extra protection.

War shields were made from the thick skin on the neck of the buffalo. To make the hide stronger, it was shrunk with steam made by splashing water on red-hot stones. Shields were usually protected by soft buckskin covers with painted designs that fitted over the thick rawhide. Before removing the cover, a Crow chief would burn wild carrot root over live coals, hold his shield above the fire and lift it four times.

The shield below belonged to Arapoosh, a Crow chief. The design represents the moon, which came to the chief disguised as a human. The dance shield at right, used in a warrior society ceremony, belonged to Short Bull, a famous Sioux. It is painted with a thunderbird design; the wavy lines rising from the wings symbolize thunder. This shield is made of soft buckskin stretched over a wooden hoop. Shields carried in dances were lighter and thinner than those carried in war.

Museum of the American Indian,
Heye Foundation

28

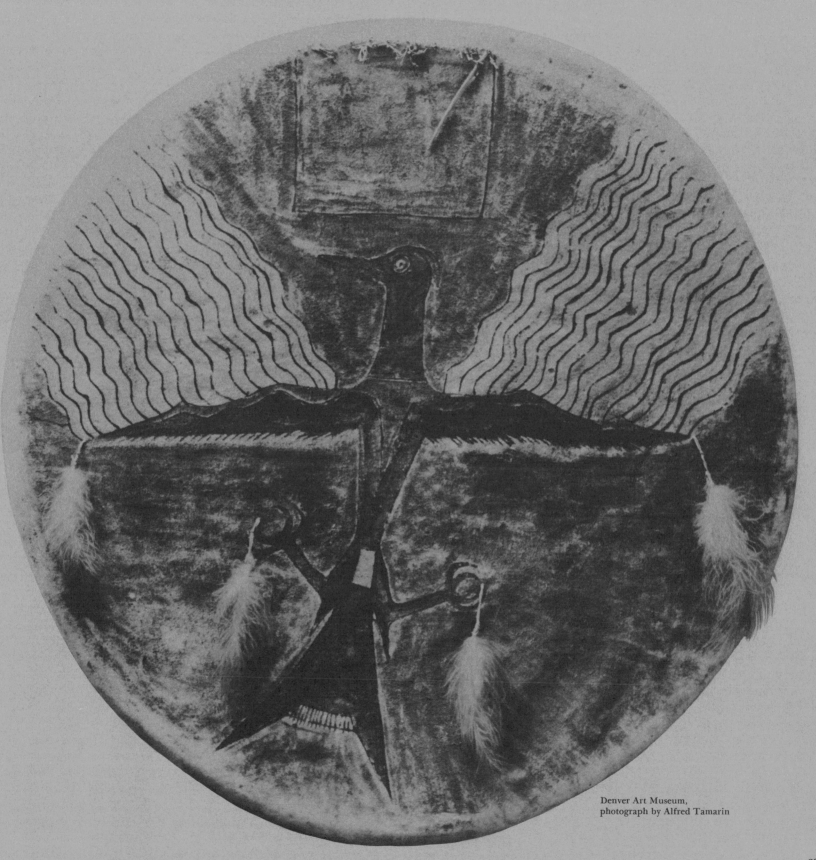

Denver Art Museum,
photograph by Alfred Tamarin

To bring success in the buffalo hunt, Mandan warriors performed dances with shields, wearing buffalo-head masks or horned headdresses. Masks were seldom worn by the Plains Indians, who rarely disguised themselves to impersonate supernatural beings as did most other North American Indian tribes.

Lances, guns and war clubs are carried by the dancers, above. Lances were often used for hunting, but only certain important warriors used them in battle. For both hunting and war a short bow and arrow, which was easy to manage on horseback, was a favorite. The beaded Blackfeet staff below, called a coup stick, was used to touch a live enemy without harming him. A *coup,* the French word for "strike," was

Glenbow-Alberta Institute

considered the bravest act in battle. Brave deeds in war brought the highest honor to a Plains Indian. A Blackfeet song says: "It is bad to live to be old. Better to die young fighting bravely in battle." A warrior would recount his war deeds on public occasions.

Simple stone clubs were used for close combat in war. Clubs carved into beautiful forms were used for trade and in victory dances. All hunting and war equipment was made by men.

Sioux, University of Colorado Museum, photograph by Alfred Tamarin

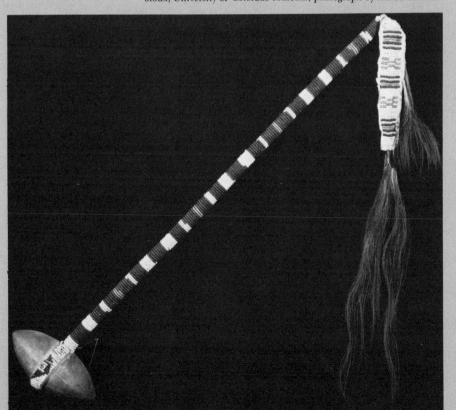

Sioux, Denver Art Museum, photograph by Alfred Tamarin

144109

Among the Plains Indians, pipes were smoked both for pleasure and for ceremonies. They were considered religious objects with magic powers. A pipe was always smoked when pledges were made. In every religious ceremony and before any battle was undertaken, a pipe was passed around.

The bowls were usually made of pipestone, called catlinite after George Catlin, an American painter. Pipestone, which is found in the Upper Missouri River region, is soft enough to be easily carved when it is first quarried. When exposed to the air, it hardens. The Indian carver smoothed the surface of the pipe bowl. Then it was greased and held over a burning fire of sage plants. Finally, it

was rubbed by hand to a fine shine. A long wooden stem was attached to the bowl.

Kee-a-kee-ka-sa-coo-way, "The Man That Gives the War Whoop," head chief of the Crees, had eleven medicine pipe stems. He used these in a ceremony to urge his men to join him in a battle to avenge warriors who had been killed in former wars. The medicine pipe he is holding in this portrait has the entire head of an eagle on the stem.

Paul Kane, about 1850, Royal Ontario Museum, Toronto

To a Plains Indian, "medicine" is a supernatural or mysterious force that gives him powers. The powers can help in the hunt, in war or even in a sport. An object that has these powers is also called "medicine." When not in use the medicine object is kept in a "bundle," a skin or cloth wrapping, with herbs such as sage and wild peony and all kinds of different charms. Medicine bundles are opened and transferred with great ceremony.

Medicine pipe, Crow,
Denver Art Museum,
photograph by
Alfred Tamarin

A Blackfeet legend tells that the original medicine pipe bundle was given to people by Thunder. A great storm was threatening, which frightened everyone. A beautiful girl, the only daughter of a chief, told Thunder she would marry him if he would take away the storm. Thunder appeared as a man and took her to the sky. After a while she grew lonely for her father. Thunder allowed her to return to him, sending him a pipestem as a gift. Since then, after the first thunder is heard each spring, medicine pipe bundles are opened with proper ceremonies.

At right, a bundle-opening ceremony is taking place in a Blackfeet medicine lodge. Items in a Blackfeet pipe bundle include a pipe with a decorated ceremonial stem, a pipe with a plain stem that can be smoked, a long whistle and the stuffed skins of animals. During the ceremony, these things are set on wooden supports made of three sticks in front of an altar, a place set aside for arranging sacred objects. Hot coals are taken from the fire and put on the altar. Sweet grass and pine needles are sprinkled on the coals to make incense, to purify the bundle. Also needed for the ceremony are a piece of buffalo-hide rope, a whip, four drums, necklaces, wristlets, a fringed bag containing paints for facial painting, and a wooden bowl for serving soup made of mashed service berries.

This ceremony took place in Alberta in the early twentieth century. Plains Indians in Canada kept their old customs longer than those in the United States because the Canadian government did not interfere as much as the American.

Early twentieth century, Provincial Archives of Alberta,
H. Pollard Collection, Edmonton, Alberta

1912,
Provincial
Archives of
Alberta,
H. Pollard
Collection

Medicine bundles were usually tubular or rectangular in shape and had long fringes. When not in use they were hung outdoors on wooden tripods in back of the tipi from daybreak until sunset, then brought indoors and hung up when night fell or if a storm approached. It was forbidden for the medicine bundle to touch the ground, except in a ceremony.

At left, Calf Child, a Blackfeet, stands in front of his medicine bundles behind his tipi at a Sun Dance. Owning a bundle is said to bring long life, success and happiness.

A Sun Dance, the most important religious ceremony on the Plains, was held in midsummer. At this time all the wandering bands in the tribe who had been chasing the buffalo herds all year came together. Friendships were renewed and information was exchanged about the best hunting territories. During the ceremony, the dancers sought visions that would foretell the future or guide them to success in life.

The contents of an open Crow medicine bundle containing a Sun Dance doll are shown at right. Crow dancers believed the Sun Dance doll held great supernatural power, and they needed to gaze at it to have a vision.

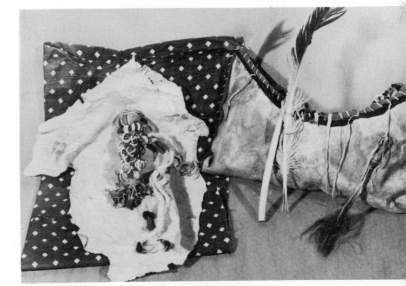

Denver Art Museum, photograph by Alfred Tamarin

Blackfeet, Provincial Museum of Alberta, photograph by Alfred Tamarin

To prepare for the Sun Dance, several medicine men used their powers to make certain that the weather would be good. Prayers were said and songs were sung as a tall tree was cut down for the sacred pole and carried to the holy ground. Before it was set up, a bundle of brush, a buffalo hide and offerings were set into a fork of this tree to symbolize an eagle's or thunderbird's nest, and colored cloth was tied around it.

People brought in leafy cottonwood branches to build the circular enclosure, which always opened toward the east, the direction of the sunrise. Meanwhile, warriors beat hand drums and everyone sang songs together. When the medicine lodge was finished, a long procession of warriors and young women rode their horses in pairs slowly around the entire camp circle until after sundown. For days people sang and did a simple dance, rising on their toes while blowing on whistles and gazing at the top of the central pole, praying for power.

Buffalo skulls that had been bleached in the sun were painted with designs representing prayers. They were stuffed with prairie grass and carefully arranged on the Sun Dance altar, which was in a clear spot within the sacred enclosure.

In the painting below, by Short Bull, an Oglala Sioux chief, the encampment of tipis has formed around the sacred enclosure and the Sun Dance is in progress. The man in the center foreground has cords attached to openings in the skin on his back. The cords are tied to buffalo skulls that he will drag until they tear loose.

About 1890, American Museum of Natural History

Painful physical ordeals were practiced during the Sun Dance by several groups of Plains Indians. Young men who had received supernatural aid in a time of danger would give thanks by taking part in these ordeals. The purpose was to have a vision.

Before seeking a vision or taking part in an important ceremony, the Indians often fasted and purified themselves. Some tribes considered it necessary to sweat for purification. The sweating took place in a sweat lodge built of willow branches. Red-hot rocks were placed in a clear space and water was sprinkled on them, causing steam. Afterward, the people cooled off in a creek.

During the Sun Dance, men who had vowed the painful ordeals had slits cut into the skin on their chests or backs. Sticks were inserted in these holes and attached

Museum of the
American Indian,
Heye Foundation

by long ropes to a pole. The men pulled against these ropes, trying to tear free, until the sticks ripped off. All the while they gazed steadily at the sun and blew whistles made of eagle bone. Because of this practice, which is known as the "making of a brave," the Sun Dance was outlawed by both the United States and Canadian governments. But now it is allowed again, and the Sun Dance is practiced today by some tribes.

The Sun Dance scene below is by Short Bull. The painting at left is by a Shoshone artist. The lower part represents the vision that was seen during the ceremony. Both paintings were made with watercolors on sheets of cotton probably issued by the United States government to Indians who were living on reservations.

About 1890, American Museum of Natural History

In the early part of the nineteenth century, Indians from the eastern United States were forced by the federal government to settle in the West on lands that were thought to be so vast and so distant they would never be needed. However, as the rush of white settlement increased and the railroads that eventually reached across the continent were built, the Plains Indians found themselves with less and less room to hunt, and life became more and more difficult. The Indians resented being pushed off their land and resisted federal troops who moved in to keep them under control. Bloody battles were fought.

Battle of the Little Big Horn, by Kicking Bear, Sioux, about 1898, Southwest Museum, Los Angeles

Reno's Retreat (detail), 1894-1895, West Point
Museum Collections, U.S. Military Academy

In Montana on the banks of the Little Big Horn River in 1876, Lieutenant Colonel

George A. Custer attacked a large encampment of Sioux and Cheyenne. Under the

leadership of Gall, Crazy Horse and Sitting Bull, the Indians defeated Custer and

killed him and about 225 of his men. The Battle of the Little Big Horn was a popular

subject for Indian artists. Years after it was over, White Bird, a Cheyenne who fought in the battle as a young man, painted the scene at left. One of the cavalry detachments is retreating from the conflict.

Now the United States government made an even greater effort to clear all Indians off the Plains. Although most of them were already settled on reservations, the government put constant pressure on them to sell what was left of their land, and cut their food rations so that the Indian people were hungry. As a last desperate attempt to resist the white people, the Ghost Dance religion was introduced on the Plains. Below is a painted cape worn in the Ghost Dance.

Sioux, Museum of the American Indian, Heye Foundation

Ghost Dance shirt,
Arapaho, Chandler
Pohrt Collection,
Great Lakes Indian
Museum, Cross
Village, Michigan

This religion gave the Indians hope that they could again be together with loved ones who had died, and that the ghosts of their ancestors could help to bring back the buffalo. During the Ghost Dance, people fasted and danced in a circle with slow steps, singing. "Mother, oh, come back. Little Brother calls as he seeks thee, weeping. Mother, oh, come back, saith the Father" was a Sioux song.

The dancers continued until they were exhausted and fell into a trance. On awaking, they described the visions that had come to them. They painted these visions on shirts and dresses. The designs were believed to protect the wearer from white men's bullets.

The whites were alarmed at the news that the Indians were meeting and dancing. In 1890 they attempted to arrest Sitting Bull, a Sioux chief, who was killed when he resisted. This event led to a massacre at Wounded Knee Creek on the Pine Ridge Reservation in South Dakota. The United States cavalry killed more than two hundred Sioux men, women and children. This massacre ended the Sioux Ghost Dance. The Indians of the Great Plains were finally subdued.

Sioux, Milwaukee Public Museum

Peyote fan, Kiowa, University of Colorado
Museum, photograph by Alfred Tamarin

Another Indian religion reached the Plains in the late nineteenth century. The Peyote religion, also called the Native American Church, includes both Indian and Christian beliefs. Meetings, which start at sundown and last until sunrise, are usually held in a tipi. The men who take part say prayers and each sings four songs; four is sacred to many Indians. They shake feather fans and rattles with beaded handles and smoke hand-rolled cigarettes. To seek a vision they eat the round tops of the peyote cactus, which has been gathered with ceremony, then dried. At midnight a special sweetened water is drunk and in the morning a ceremonial breakfast is eaten. The Peyote religion is very popular and is still growing.

The Plains Indian days of glory lasted only about two hundred years. Gone are the buffalo and their vast grazing lands. For some time the old practices were almost forgotten. But today many young Plains Indians are interested in the old culture. They are trying to bring back their ancient traditions and make them a part of their lives.

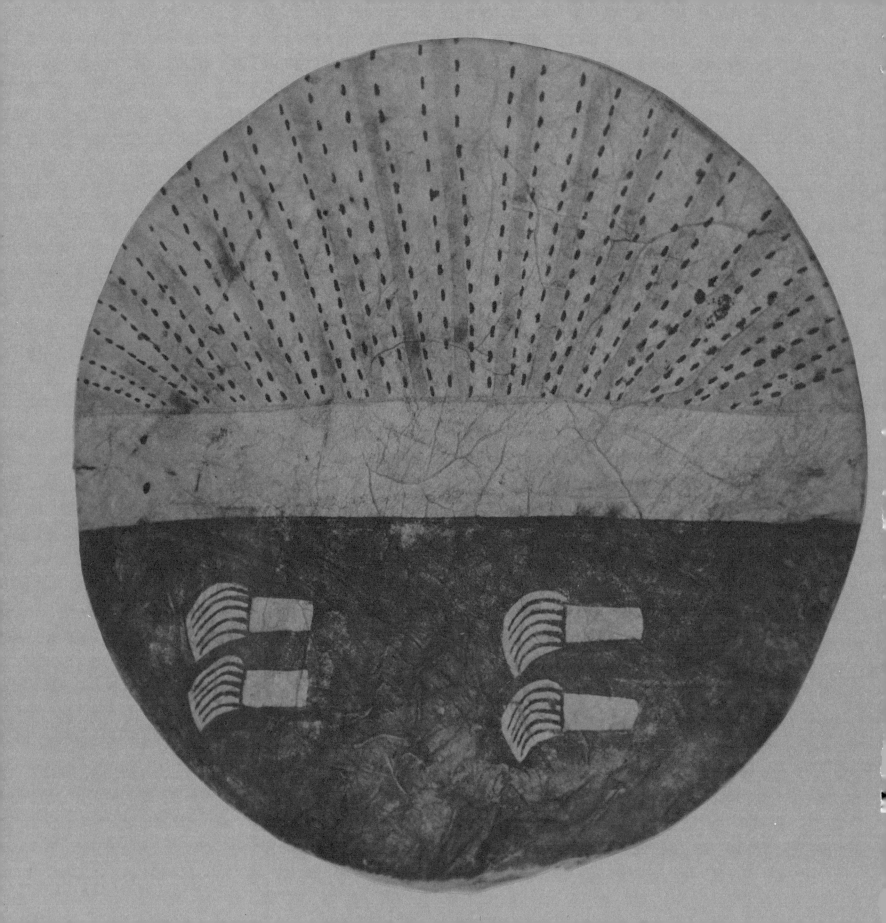